Stars, Stockings & Shepherds

D1191613

Discover the meaning of **CHRISTMAS** Symbols

Stars, Stockings & Shepherds

Written by **Shersta Chabot**

Illustrated by **Corey Egbert**

CFI
An Imprint of Cedar Fort, Inc.
Springville, Utah

Pender County Public Library
POB 879 Burgaw, NC 28425
910-259-1234
103 S. Cowan Street

Text © 2014 Shersta Chabot
Illustrations © 2014 Corey Egbert
All rights reserved.

No part of this book may be reproduced in any form whatsoever, whether by graphic, visual, electronic, film, microfilm, tape recording, or any other means, without prior written permission of the publisher, except in the case of brief passages embodied in critical reviews and articles.

This is not an official publication of The Church of Jesus Christ of Latter-day Saints. The opinions and views expressed herein belong solely to the author and do not necessarily represent the opinions or views of Cedar Fort, Inc. Permission for the use of sources, graphics, and photos is also solely the responsibility of the author.

ISBN 978-1-4621-1462-7

Published by CFI, an imprint of Cedar Fort, Inc.
2373 W. 700 S., Springville, UT 84663
Distributed by Cedar Fort, Inc., www.cedarfort.com

The Library of Congress has cataloged the first edition, The Symbols of Christmas, as follows:

Chabot, Shersta, 1976- author.
Symbols of Christmas : a day-by-day celebration of the meaning of the holiday / Shersta Chabot.
pages cm
ISBN 978-1-4621-1087-2
1. Christmas. I. Title.

GT4985.C43 2012
394.2663--dc23

2012026269

Cover and interior layout design by Shawnda T. Craig
Cover design © 2014 Lyle Mortimer
Edited by Jessica B. Ellingson

Printed in China

10 9 8 7 6 5 4 3 2 1

To my extraordinary three,
Erin, Makenna, and Isaac,
who give meaning to my life
and teach love to my heart.
—Shersta Chabot

To my family.
—Corey Egbert

Have you ever looked at...

a Christmas tree, a stocking, or a pretty bow, and wondered why these things are a part of the holidays? Christmastime is filled with things that we don't often see the rest of the year: ornaments, candy canes, colored lights, and the baby Jesus in a manger. Remembering Jesus's birth, or *Nativity*, is the reason that we celebrate Christmas each year. The Nativity, sweet treats, gifts, and family traditions are all part of what makes Christmas so special. But did you know that many of these things have hidden meanings? Twinkling lights and bright stars and shiny bows and kneeling shepherds—all of these things are symbols. By learning about Christmas symbols and their meanings, we can discover the many ways that God shows His love for each one of us. We can discover messages that are hidden, in plain sight, in our favorite parts of the holidays.

TREES

Most Christmas trees are *evergreens*, or trees that stay green even in the cold of winter. In order to grow tall, evergreen trees must stand strong through many storms. They are a symbol of strength and of standing firm in your beliefs, and of keeping your promises, even when it is hard to do so. The top of the evergreen tree reaches up into the sky, reminding us of heaven and of the loving God who is waiting for us there.

Lights

At Christmastime, we often have colorful lights and candles that decorate our homes and trees. In the scriptures, Jesus is called the Light of the World. This is because He brought the "light" of knowledge and truth into the world. At Christmas, lights and candles are a symbol of this divine light and the divine life of the spirit inside each one of us. Christmas lights remind us to look to Jesus for truth in all things.

Bows

At Christmastime, we can find bows and ribbons all around, decorating our trees and homes. When we give gifts to our friends and loved ones, we often decorate them with beautiful bows. Because bows are tied, they are symbols of other kinds of ties, like the ties of love between parents, children, and families. Christmas bows help us to remember that we are all children of a Heavenly Father, who loves us.

GIFTS

Giving a gift is an act of love. When Jesus was born, the Wise Men brought gifts to honor Him. When Jesus died, He gave us all the gift of everlasting life because He loves us. When we give gifts to each other at Christmas, they become symbols of the love of Jesus. Gifts help us to remember to honor Jesus like the Wise Men did.

CAROLS

The word caroling comes from the Italian word *carolare*. In the old days, caroling meant singing and dancing around the Christmas tree. These kinds of songs and dances weren't holy enough to sing inside of a church, so caroling was done outside—and often still is today! The scriptures tell us that it is good for us to sing. When we sing Christmas songs about Jesus, we remember the miracle of His birth. Caroling or singing is one way that we can show our love for Jesus.

WREATHS

In ancient Greece, athletes who came in first place in the Olympic games were given special wreaths that they would hang on walls or doors. In Scandinavian countries, a wreath with candles is worn as part of the celebration of Saint Lucia. The circle shape of the wreath is a symbol of something that has no beginning or end. The Christmas wreath is a symbol of God's love for us, which is eternal, or lasts forever, and like a circle, has no beginning or end.

ST. NicHoLAS

St. Nicholas, also known as Santa Claus, is a jolly, magical old man who leaves gifts for good girls and boys. While Santa Claus might look a little different or be called by a different name, he is always a symbol of the spirit of *generosity*, or giving without expecting anything in return. St. Nicholas reminds us that it is good to give to others freely, and to treat others with kindness and with love.

REINDEER

The reindeer is a strong animal that lives in the cold lands of the north. Reindeer wear a thick coat of fur and have large antlers. In many of the Christmas stories about St. Nicholas, reindeer pull a sleigh that is filled with gifts for others. Because of their strength and kind service, reindeer are a symbol of serving others. They remind us that we must use our own strengths, and do whatever we can do, for those around us.

Pender County Public Library
POB 879 Burgaw, NC 28425
910-259-1234
103 S. Cowan Street

STOCKINGS

An old story tells about a kind man with three daughters. They were very poor and worked very hard. One evening, the daughters washed their stockings and hung them to dry near the fireplace. St. Nicholas came in the night and secretly placed a bag of gold into each stocking. Children have hung stockings at Christmastime ever since. Stockings are a symbol of giving. They remind us to give with our whole hearts, whether we are recognized for it or not.

CANDY CANES

The shape of a candy cane looks like the shape of a shepherd's staff. A shepherd's staff has a crook on one end, which the shepherd can use to help guide lost sheep back to the safety of the flock. In the scriptures, Jesus is compared to a shepherd, searching for those who are lost and gently leading them to safety. The candy cane is a symbol of the love of Jesus, our Shepherd, who was born to show us the way to get back home to heaven.

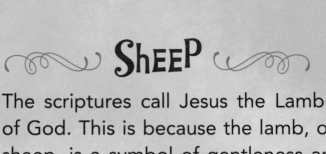

Sheep

The scriptures call Jesus the Lamb of God. This is because the lamb, or sheep, is a symbol of gentleness and patience. It is also a symbol of purity and sacrifice. Jesus was gentle, patient, and pure. At Christmas, the sheep or lamb reminds us to sacrifice, or give up, the things we do wrong so that we can be more like Him.

ShePheRDs

A shepherd keeps sheep safe and shows them the way to go. In the scriptures, Jesus is called the Good Shepherd because He was sent to guide us back to our Heavenly Father. In ancient times, the shepherd was a symbol of sacred kingship. In the scriptures, many of the great prophets were shepherds before becoming great leaders. At Christmastime, the shepherd is a symbol of a kind and loving leader who, like Jesus, guides us in the way that we should go.

HOLLY

Holly is a plant with spiny leaves and clusters of red berries. Its glossy leaves stay green all year, even during the winter. The pretty green and red colors make it a favorite decoration for Christmastime. Holly is a symbol of good fortune, or luck. In the past, people thought that if you hung branches of holly on doors and windows, it would invite good luck in and keep the bad luck out. Hanging holly on a door also shows that the birth of Christ is celebrated in that home.

RED

At Christmastime, we see the color red everywhere, from bows and lights to the color of Santa's suit. The color red is a symbol of riches, and also a symbol of royalty. In the scriptures, Jesus is called the Prince of Peace, and so He is often shown in paintings wearing red clothing. The color red is also a symbol of the heart and feelings of love. At Christmas, the color red can remind us of the love that Jesus has for us, and that we should love Him in return.

DRUMS

The song "Little Drummer Boy" tells the story of a young boy who wanted to give a gift to the baby Jesus, but all he had was a drum. The little boy decided to play his drum for Jesus, and this song became the boy's gift. At Christmas, the drum is a symbol of giving of ourselves. The sound of a drum is like the sound of a heartbeat, which reminds us to give from the heart. Drums remind us to use our talents, whatever they might be, and to give of what we have to others.

BELLS

Bells have many uses. They ring to remind people to come to church, to warn of danger, or to celebrate happy events and holidays, like Christmas. In the same way that bells have many uses, they also have many meanings. Bells are a symbol of creativity and of harmony. They are a symbol of *communication*, or prayers, between God and His children. Bells remind us to pray to our Heavenly Father and to listen for when He calls us to come unto Him.

❧ Wise Men ☙

Long ago, prophecy told of the coming of a Messiah and a new star that would appear as a sign of His birth. Men of science studied the night skies, and when the star finally appeared, they followed it to Bethlehem. At Christmas, these Wise Men are shown as three kings bringing gifts of gold, frankincense, and myrrh. The Wise Men are a symbol of the divine and royal nature of God's children. They remind us of the importance of following the light of truth back to Jesus.

GOLD

Gold can be both a color and an object. Usually, gold represents something of great value. But gold can also symbolize power, strength, and justice. Kings often wear gold to show that they are powerful, strong and *just*, or fair. Gold was one of the gifts that the Wise Men brought to Jesus. Gold reminds us of the valuable gifts of love and eternal life that Jesus has given to us. It also helps us remember that we must give Him something of great value in return.

STARS

When Jesus was born, shepherds and wise men followed a new star to Bethlehem, where He lay in a manger. Stars like this one are symbols of wisdom or guides. Long ago, stars were believed to appear when important people, like kings, were born. Because a new star appeared when Jesus was born, Christmas stars remind us of Him.

DOVES

The dove is a bird with pure white feathers. In the scriptures, the Holy Spirit appears in the shape of a dove. The dove can be a symbol for gentleness and for purity. At Christmastime, the dove is a symbol of the spirit of peace. It reminds us to keep the spirit of peace in our hearts. The dove also reminds us to follow the gentle guidance of the Holy Spirit, just like Jesus did.

MARY

Mary is the mother of Jesus. The scriptures tell us that Mary was "highly favored" for her faith in God. Mary received a visit from the angel Gabriel, who told her that she had been chosen to be the mother of the Savior of the world. She travelled to Bethlehem with Joseph and gave birth to Jesus. She was also there when Jesus died. She cared for Jesus His entire life. At Christmastime, Mary is a symbol of a faithful mother's courage and love.

JOSEPH

Joseph was the husband of Mary, and a descendant of King David. In the scriptures, Joseph is described as "a just man." This means that he was honest and fair. Joseph received a personal revelation from God before the birth of Jesus, and then again when the lives of his family were in danger. Because he listened to this message, he kept his family safe. Jesus always showed His love and respect for Joseph. At Christmas, Joseph is a symbol of righteous fatherhood.

ANGELS

In the scriptures, angels are messengers from heaven that often bring joyful news. Sometimes angels appear surrounded by a bright white light, even at night. Angels told Mary and Joseph of their calling to be the earthly parents of Jesus. Angels announced the birth of Jesus to the shepherds. The angel is a symbol for dignity, glory, and honor. At Christmastime, the angel reminds us that we are watched over by a loving Heavenly Father.

∾❀◇ JESUS ◇❀∾

Born of an earthly mother and our Heavenly Father, Jesus is both our brother and our Savior. He gave His life so that we could live together forever. It is His birth we celebrate at Christmastime. Jesus is a symbol for many things, but at Christmas, it is His perfect love for us that we remember most.

ABOUT THE AUTHOR

SHERSTA CHABOT

grew up in Utah, the oldest in a family of eleven children. After starting a family and working for several years in both corporate and small business accounting, she returned to her first love—English literature—and completed her bachelor's degree while working as an acquisitions editor for a local trade publishing company. Currently, she lives in Phoenix, Arizona, with her three children, where she has taken on the challenges of author, graduate student, and college writing teacher. Shersta is the author of *Till We Meet Again* and *Angels of Christmas*.

ABOUT THE ILLUSTRATOR

COREY EGBERT

is a husband to an amazing wife, father to a super-cute little boy, and a humble subject to his cat, Rex. He can often be found taking pictures of run-down old buildings, obsessively reading books and blogs about art, and (secretly) watching documentaries about cheese. He loves illustrating and is still amazed that he gets to do it as a real job. He currently lives with his family in Virginia.

0 26575 14627 1